NATURE'S ULTIMATE DISASTERS

TOP 10 WORST

WILDFIRES

Louise and Richard Spilsbury

PowerKiDS press.
New York

Published in 2017 by
The Rosen Publishing Group, Inc.
29 East 21st Street, New York, NY 10010

Cataloging-in-Publication Data

Names: Spilsbury, Louise.
Title: Top 10 worst wildfires / Louise and Richard Spilsbury.
Description: New York : PowerKids Press, 2017. | Series: Nature's ultimate disasters | Includes index.
Identifiers: ISBN 9781499430691 (pbk.) | ISBN 9781499430714 (library bound) | ISBN 9781499430707 (6 pack)
Subjects: LCSH: Wildfires--Juvenile literature.
Classification: LCC SD421.23 S65 2017 | DDC 363.34'9--dc23

Produced for Rosen by Calcium
Editors for Calcium Creative Ltd: Sarah Eason and Harriet McGregor
Designers: Paul Myerscough and Simon Borrough
Picture research: Rachel Blount

Picture credits: Cover: Shutterstock: Nico Jacobs; Inside: Alamy: Forget Patrick/Sagaphoto.com 13; Library of Congress: Posters of the WPA/Christopher DeNoon. Los Angeles: Wheatly Press, c1987, no. 230 21t; National Archives of Australia: A6135, K1/3/83/114 11; Shutterstock: Vladimir Daragan 23, Evgenia Sh. 9, Chokchai Poomichaiya 27, Myszka 15, Tom Reichner 4–5, Toa55 7t, Ververidis Vasilis 1, 6–7, Serg Zastavkin 19; Wikimedia Commons: The New York Public Library 17, P199 21. Self 25.

Manufactured in the United States of America
CPSIA Compliance Information: Batch #BW17PK: For Further Information contact Rosen Publishing, New York, New York at 1-800-237-9932.

Contents

WILDFIRE DANGER

Fire is one of the greatest threats to the world's forests. Fires can spread quickly through wooded areas, destroying everything in their path. Forest fires can move so fast and so violently that they also threaten homes and lives.

How Dangerous?

Some forest fires can be easily contained. Firefighters put them out before they cause too much damage. Large forest fires destroy important wildlife **habitats** and kill animals. People often escape in time but some get injured or killed by the flames or by falling trees. Large forest fires can burn for days or weeks, producing a lot of smoke that can affect people's breathing or even **suffocate** them if it fills their lungs.

Measuring Disaster

Scientists and firefighters are working on ways to predict when and where forest fires will happen and how to stop fires.

Fires happen when it is hot and dry. They spread with the wind.

Weather forecasters use **satellite** images to predict where lightning might start a fire and where hot temperatures, dry weather, and high winds create fire hazards.

Forest fires spread fast and far because dry plants and plant waste catch alight easily.

Firefighters clear a wide line of plants and plant waste at the edge of a forest. When a fire reaches this **firebreak** it stops.

Fires in remote places are difficult to fight.

Some firefighters drop water or chemicals from helicopters or planes to put out fires.

It can take forests a very long time to recover from a fire. Some of the oldest trees that burned down may be hundreds of years old.

Natural disasters have taken place since Earth was formed. People have many ways of deciding what the world's worst natural disasters have been, from the deadliest disaster to the costliest. This book includes some of the worst disasters in history.

WILDFIRES IN ACTION

Forest fires start in different ways and for different reasons. In most cases, forest fires are caused by people. Either through an accident, a mistake, or purposely, humans create the sparks that cause the worst forest blazes.

Starting Fires

People sometimes start forest fires when sparks from machinery, a campfire, or a fire used to burn and clear land of vegetation blows out of control. Sometimes a careless action such as dropping a cigarette from a car window can start a fire. **Arson** is when someone deliberately starts a fire to cause trouble. Wind can fan small fires, making them bigger and spreading them quickly. The wind can also blow sparks or **embers** onto new plants, starting new fires.

Strong winds can force forest fires to change direction, making the fires even more dangerous and unpredictable.

In Greece in 2007, firefighters had to fight hard to keep forest fires from spreading to the capital city, Athens.

Heat and Drought

Many forest fires happen after a heat wave, which is a long period of very hot weather. **Drought** makes the land and plants in an area dry and warm. They then catch alight much more easily if touched by a spark. When a small area of dry grass catches alight, for example, the fire heats any surrounding dry plants even more so sparks can easily set them alight, too.

Fire Creating Fire

As a fire grows bigger, it becomes more and more powerful. It creates so much heat and energy that it spreads faster and farther, and consumes even more plants and trees. Forest fires can even create their own winds. When fires heat the air above the ground, the air rises, forming winds.

10 RUSSIA

In 2010, the hottest summer in Russian history fueled hundreds of fires across the country. The catastrophic fires burned around 3,000 square miles (7,800 sq km) of land and turned the skies dark. The fires themselves killed at least 54 people but no one really knows how many more died as a result of the smoke pollution.

Russia

Widespread Fires

The average maximum July temperature for Moscow is around 73 degrees Fahrenheit (23° C). In 2010, some regions experienced temperatures up to 111 degrees Fahrenheit (44° C). The high temperatures combined with a severe drought and strong winds whipped up and spread smaller fires that were mostly caused by carelessness, such as dropping cigarettes in dense woodlands. There were nearly 600 fires in total. They started burning in late July and lasted until early September. The fires spread close to towns and cities. Smoke trapped everyone indoors, leaving streets empty and schools closed.

On the Record

At least 2,000 homes were destroyed in the fires.

Russia used over 200,000 firefighters, 30,000 trucks and engines, and about 200 aircraft to fight the fires.

The smoke cloaked several cities for weeks, causing unhealthy levels of smoke and **smog**.

The center of Moscow, Russia's capital city, was full of smoke due to the raging wildfires of August 2010.

Smoke from forest fires around Moscow kept some planes from using the airport.

The smoke and smog made people choke and cough, made their eyes water, and caused **respiratory illnesses**.

The smoke covered streets and even got into metro stations deep underground!

9 ASH WEDNESDAY

The Australian Ash Wednesday fires that swept through parts of Victoria and South Australia on February 16, 1983, were some of the worst bushfires Australia ever experienced.

Fierce Fires

Hot and dry summers make fire a real risk in Victoria's forests of eucalyptus trees. By February 1983, the area had suffered 10 months of drought: its driest period on record. Plants were dry, there were high winds, and little moisture was in the air. On Ash Wednesday, temperatures reached 109 degrees Fahrenheit (43° C). Bushfires broke out over a wide area, caused by the clashing of electric power lines, tree branches hitting power lines, by sparks from deliberate fires, and by other unknown causes.

South Australia

Victoria

On the Record

There were many **spot fires**, caused by burning material blown ahead of the main fire. Some spread quickly and joined to form a large fire ahead of the main fire.

A wind direction change caused fires to alter their course and merge. Most deaths occurred in the hour after the wind change.

The fires killed 75 people, including 12 firefighters, and injured and burned hundreds more. Large numbers of people fled to the beaches to escape the flames.

Around 3,000 buildings were destroyed and more than 1,000 square miles (3,000 sq km) of land were burned.

More than 16,000 firefighters and 1,000 police officers fought the fires.

8 LANDES FOREST

The most deadly fire in Europe in modern times happened in France, in August 1949. Around 500 square miles (1,300 sq km) of forest went up in smoke.

Landes forest

Highly Flammable

The Landes region in southwest France, between the Bordeaux River and the Spanish border, has a giant pine forest. The trees have a lot of **sap** called resin, which contains oils that make the trees highly **flammable**. This means they burn easily, and they are set alight especially well if they are dry. In the summer of 1949, the Landes forest was so dry that 350 fires raged. They spread partly because there were fewer people in the region after World War II (1939–1945), which meant there were not enough local firefighters. There was also too much undergrowth around the trees that should have been cleared to slow the spread of fire.

Of the 83 people who died in the Landes fire, many were volunteer firefighters and soldiers brought in from across France to stop the blaze.

The Landes forest was made by people. They planted maritime pine trees because they grow well in the warm, moist climate near the ocean.

Settlements including Arcachon, Cestas, and Saucats were badly damaged in the fire.

After the Landes fire, the local fire service developed better firefighting techniques. Now they can put out a 5 acre (2 ha) fire in less than 5 minutes.

Today, firefighters react immediately to fires in the Landes forest and quickly put them out.

13

7 BLACK SATURDAY

On February 2, 2009, a series of bushfires swept across the state of Victoria in Australia. These fierce and incredibly hot fires were so deadly that the day became known as "Black Saturday."

Heat Wave!

Victoria was experiencing a record-breaking heat wave that February, with temperatures up to 115.5 degrees Fahrenheit (46.4° C). The area had been suffering a long, harsh drought that had dried out a lot of the plants. This made them much more likely to catch alight. In this extreme heat, 47 major fires started. They spread across the state quickly because powerful winds blew huge balls of flames called **fireballs** through trees and towns.

Victoria

On the Record

The flames were so hot, their heat could kill people from 980 feet (300 m) away.

The fires created winds of 75 miles (120 km) per hour that snapped trees in half. Flames leaped 330 feet (100 m) into the air.

One fire started with a faulty power pole 37 miles (60 km) north of Melbourne. Wind blew the flames into a forest, and on through towns, killing people in their homes.

Some people tried to escape the fires by car, but the flames moved so fast many died on the roads.

The fires killed 173 people and injured 500 more. They destroyed thousands of homes.

Some people died because they stayed in their homes, hoping to protect them. They also thought they would be safe there.

6 MIRAMICHI

The great Miramichi fire happened on October 7, 1825, in New Brunswick, Canada. This fire destroyed 6,000 square miles (16,000 sq km) of land in just 8 hours.

Miramichi

Fire Conditions

The summer of 1825 had been very warm with little rain. Forests in the Miramichi area were already vulnerable, too, that summer as many trees had died from insect damage. Most Miramichi buildings were made out of wood harvested from the huge surrounding forest. Conditions were perfect for fires. A large one broke out in a forest in northwestern Miramichi, where William Wright was working. He ran into the biggest local town, Newcastle, warning people to flee by beating a drum. Unfortunately, no one reacted: they thought it was just a thunderstorm.

On the Record

The violently strong winds on October 7 made the fire burn at 1 mile (1.6 km) per minute.

Many ships moored on the north shore of the Miramichi River were burned. Some escaping ships accidentally carried the flames to the south shore.

This drawing shows Miramichi in the late eighteenth century. By 1825, the settlements along the Miramichi River had grown bigger due to wealth from selling wood and animal skins from the forest.

To escape the heat of the fire, many people stood in the river up to their necks.

Heavy rain, on October 8, doused the fire. By then, 520 buildings had been destroyed.

Heat from the fire was so intense that it baked potatoes growing underground in the fields!

5 BLACK DRAGON

The Black Dragon Forest got its name because it is a dark, densely packed area of coniferous trees cloaking a mountain range. This fire was the worst fire in China for 300 years. It burned an area of forest the size of New England, in the United States.

Black Dragon Forest

A Wall of Fire

In May 1987, conditions in the Black Dragon were unusually dry. There had been little snowfall the previous winter and low rainfall during spring. High winds fanned several small fires, which had started accidentally. The fires spread through the forest and joined together, forming an enormous wall of fire. The Black Dragon fire was at its most terrifying on the night of May 7, when over 200 people died, mostly from smoke fumes. Another 250 people were seriously injured.

On the Record

The advancing fire was so intense that it used up a lot of **oxygen** in the air as it burned more and more wood. Truck engines stopped working because there was not enough oxygen to burn the fuel.

On the Chinese side of the Amur River, 60,000 soldiers and forest workers tackled the blaze. They wanted to protect their country's **timber**.

On the Russian side of the river, the forest was left to burn because authorities thought they had plenty more trees in other forests.

Many animals died or lost vital habitat in the Black Dragon fire, including many Amur leopards.

Around 58,000 square miles (150,000 sq km) of mountainous forest were destroyed.

MATHESON

The 1916 Matheson fire in Ontario was probably Canada's worst ever. This raging inferno measured 40 miles (64 km) across and moved at 40 miles (64 km) per hour through the forest.

Matheson

Frontier Lands

The railroad was built up to Cochrane, Ontario, in 1908, and settlers moved into the area all around. They cleared forest to sell and make things from timber, but also to create space for farms and settlements. This left enormous amounts of "slash," or unwanted branches, thin tree trunks, and other waste on the forest floor. On July 29, 1916, the settlers' usual practice of burning the slash to remove it went horribly wrong. The forest was very dry and conditions were windy, and the fires spread rapidly.

On the Record

The death toll of the Matheson fire was at least 223.

The Matheson fire was so terrible that for several days it shared Canadian newspaper headlines with news about World War I (1914–1918) raging in Europe.

The fire changed Canadian law. By 1917, Ontario had produced the Forest Fires Prevention Act. This forced people to prevent, be prepared for, and know how to stop future fires.

The fire burned through timber yards and destroyed an area of 800 square miles (2,000 sq km).

People failed to control the blaze and it only stopped during rainfall in early August.

The Matheson fire completely destroyed seven settlements, including Matheson and Cochrane, and partly destroyed a number of others.

3 CLOQUET

The Cloquet-Moose Lake forest fires that occurred in northeastern Minnesota in 1918 became a devastating natural disaster. The fires spread easily through dry tree stumps and waste that remained after pine forests had been cut down for wood.

Cloquet

Forest on Fire

The fires came at the end of a long, hot summer of drought. Trees and stored timber in the area were a **tinderbox** waiting to catch fire. There were already several small fires in the area, when on October 12, sparks from train engines started fires in dry brush next to the tracks. Strong winds blew the flames, and the fires joined to become enormous. They spread to the Moose Lake-Kettle River area, killing a total of 453 people. Eighty-five more people were badly burned and 2,100 were injured.

On the Record

The fires lasted 15 hours but moved so quickly that many people were taken by surprise.

This photo shows the forests in the Moose Lake region today. The fires damaged 1,500 square miles (4,000 sq km) of this land in Minnesota.

More than 52,000 people lost their homes and all their belongings in the fire.

Thousands of farms and farm animals were lost.

Smoke from the fires obscured the sun throughout the midwestern and eastern states for several days.

Some people survived by covering themselves with wet dirt in farm fields. Other people sheltered in wells, streams, lakes, or cellars.

2 PESHTIGO

The Peshtigo fire, of 1871, in Wisconsin is the worst forest fire recorded in North American history. Reports vary but it is estimated to have killed between 1,200 and 2,400 people. More than 1,880 square miles (4.860 sq km) of forest were burned to the ground.

Peshtigo

A Fateful Night

There had been scattered forest fires smoldering for days when, on October 8, winds picked up that made the fires bigger and spread faster. When flames blew from the forests next to Peshtigo into the city, it was burned to the ground. The fires destroyed millions of dollars' worth of property and trees grown for timber. By coincidence, there was a great fire in the city of Chicago on the same fateful night, where 250 people died.

On the Record

Small **fire tornadoes** traveled ahead of the blaze at around 6 miles (10 km) per hour.

This mass grave at the Peshtigo Fire Cemetery is a memorial to 350 unidentified victims.

The fires created fast winds that ripped up trees, blew roofs off buildings, and blasted barns apart.

There was just one horse-drawn steam pumper for fighting fires in the area, but nothing else to help people put the huge fire out.

Many affected farms and homes were very remote. Before phones, there was no way of warning people.

When the fires reached Peshtigo, it burned quickly because of its wooden buildings and sidewalks, and sawdust-covered streets.

1 INDONESIA

In 2015, thousands of devastating forest fires burned the length and breadth of Indonesia. The fires caused huge clouds of smog that spread over parts of Southeast Asia for months.

Indonesia

Slash and Burn

Many of the fires were started by companies and farmers who use fires to burn down trees to clear areas of land. They wanted to use the land to grow palm oil trees and trees for wood pulp to make paper. However, high temperatures and drought had made the land very dry so the fires spread quickly over large areas. **Deforestation** exposes **peat** beneath the trees. Fires in peatland are very hard to put out. In 2015, the fires went on for months.

On the Record

There were around 100,000 fires in total.

In some places, people used elephants to carry water pumps and other equipment to put out fires.

The thick blanket of smog resulted in 500,000 people getting respiratory illnesses. This could cause more than 100,000 deaths.

The smoke from the fires created massive air pollution across Indonesia, Malaysia, and Singapore.

The fires devastated many of Indonesia's national parks and deep forests where threatened rare wildlife such as orangutans live.

The fires released **carbon dioxide** into the air, which contributes to **global warming**.

The fires caused billions of dollars' worth of damage.

WHERE IN THE WORLD?

This map shows the locations of the wildfires featured in this book.

Matheson

Miramichi

Cloquet

Landes forest

Peshtigo

ATLANTIC OCEAN

How do you think global warming might increase the risk of forest fires in some areas? Explain your answer.

PACIFIC OCEAN

Read the case studies about the forest fires in Indonesia in 2015, the number 1 fire in this book, and the fires in Russia in 2010, which are number 10. How do they differ?

What facts can you find in this book to support the argument that humans are a major cause of forest fire disasters?

Russia

Black Dragon

PACIFIC OCEAN

INDIAN OCEAN

Indonesia

Ash Wednesday

Describe in your own words some of the ways in which people predict fires and work to stop them causing terrible damage.

Black Saturday

GLOSSARY

arson When a fire is lit on purpose with the intention of causing damage to people, land, or property.

bushfires Uncontrolled fires in the trees and bushes of scrubland.

carbon dioxide A gas in the air that contributes to global warming.

coniferous Trees that grow their seeds in cones and have needle-like leaves. They lose and renew leaves all year-round, so always look "evergreen."

deforestation Clearing of forests.

drought Long period without rain.

embers Smoldering pieces of wood or coal from a fire.

fire tornadoes Swirling winds created by a fire and usually made up of flames or ash.

fireballs Balls of fire and fiery gas blown through the air.

firebreak A strip of land cleared of plants to stop the spread of fire.

flammable Burns easily.

global warming An increase in the temperature of Earth's atmosphere caused by human activities such as burning oil, coal, and gas.

habitats The natural homes of plants and animals.

oxygen A gas in the air that animals need to breathe.

peat Dead plants that have decayed in the ground. Peat burns easily and for long periods of time.

pollution When the environment is poisoned or harmed by human waste and activity.

respiratory illnesses Diseases to do with the lungs.

sap Fluid inside plants.

satellite An object in space that travels around Earth.

smog A fog made heavier and darker by smoke fumes.

sparks Small particles of fire thrown from a larger fire.

spot fires Fires started by flying sparks or embers at a distance from a main fire.

suffocate When someone dies because they cannot breathe.

timber Wood prepared ready to build something.

tinderbox Word used to describe a thing that will catch fire easily.

FURTHER READING

Books

Petersen, Justin. *Smokejumpers* (EMERGENCY!).
North Mankato, MN: Capstone Press, 2016.

Simon, Seymour. *Wildfires*. New York, NY: HarperCollins, 2016.

Thiessen, Mark. *Extreme Wildfire.* Washington, DC: National
Geographic Children's Books, 2016.

Websites

Due to the changing nature of Internet links, PowerKids Press
has developed an online list of websites related to the subject
of this book. This site is updated regularly. Please use this link
to access the list: **www.powerkidslinks.com/nud/wildfires**

INDEX